The Urban Environment

Prue Poulton and Gillian Symons
Photographs by Jenny Matthews
Illustrations by Peter Bull Art Studio

A & C Black · London

Contents

Cover photographs
Front – Plotting land use in the town (see page 4)
Back – Land use in Maputo (see page 4)

Title page photograph – A planned new town (see page 29)

Acknowledgements
Photographs by Jenny Matthews except for: p.6t Mansell Collection; p.6b Mark Edwards, Still Pictures; p.10tr Ed Barber; p.13 Mark Edwards, Still Pictures; p.16 Paul Trevor; pp.18, 20, 22t, 24t, 25 Mark Edwards, Still Pictures; p.29 The Creative Company/Milton Keynes Development Corporation; p.29b, 31 Mark Edwards, Still Pictures.

Illustrations by Peter Bull Art Studio.

The authors and publisher would like to thank the staff and pupils of Grasmere J.M.I. School for their invaluable help in the production of the photographs for this book, and all Hackney schools for their part in developing environmental education ideas over a period of years.

A CIP record for this book is available from the British Library.

ISBN 0-7136-3541-X

First published 1992 A & C Black (Publishers) Ltd
35 Bedford Row, London WC1R 4JH

Typeset by Rowland Phototypesetting Ltd,
Bury St Edmunds, Suffolk
Printed in Italy by Imago

Living together

Where do you live? If it is in a town or city, you are part of an urban environment. The people who live in an urban environment need housing, schools, shops, transport, places to work such as factories and offices, places of worship such as synagogues, churches and mosques and leisure facilities and open spaces where they can relax.

How do the buildings in Maputo in Mozambique compare with the ones in the place where you live?

How are the buildings used locally?

On a large scale map of your neighbourhood, mark how the buildings are used. You could choose a different colour for each kind of use, for example, housing, leisure, and so on. If you do, remember to provide a key. Which kind of use takes up the most space?

When large numbers of people live close together, the actions of just one person can have an effect on many others.

Someone playing loud music late at night can keep many people awake. One car parked across a pavement forces pedestrians to walk in the road and may cause an accident. Small pieces of litter dropped by many individuals create the big piles of rubbish seen in some cities. What other examples can you think of?

Most people agree that there have to be laws and systems for organising the ways people live together. In all democratic countries, these systems are set up by representatives elected by the people to local and national government. Find out how decisions are made in your area.

How urban areas develop

Why do you think that towns and cities grew up in the areas where they are now? Often, they developed along the path of a river or around the place where two busy roads crossed.

In Britain in the nineteenth century, many new factories were built and towns developed quickly as people came to live near the factories to find work.

Today, towns and cities still offer more jobs and places to live than country areas, so the number of people who live in urban areas is continuing to increase.

▲ In Britain in the late nineteenth century, rows of houses were built back-to-back to provide homes for factory workers. Are there any streets like these in your area?

▼ The city of Rio de Janeiro in Brazil is expanding as people move into the area to look for work.

People and Jobs

Some towns and cities grew up around one industry such as making cars or weaving cloth. Who employs the most people in your area? Carry out a survey of all the jobs done by the people you and your friends know. Make a graph of the results.

Ask older people you know if they worked in different kinds of jobs when they were young. Did they move to the area to look for work?

If you want to find out more about the history of your area, you could visit your local library. It may have an archive section with old maps, photographs and press cuttings about important local events, as well as books on local history.

Home improvements

Most people enjoy living in a well cared for, pleasant environment and want to keep it looking good. But if their surroundings are unpleasant, people often feel there is nothing they can do about it and may even add to the problem by writing graffiti or dropping litter.

Today, architects who are designing buildings often consult the people who will be living in and around these buildings. Planners sometimes hold public meetings and exhibitions to show possible changes to an area and ask for local people's reactions before they make the changes.

These pictures show the changes that were made to an apartment block after the architects had discussed their plans with the people who lived in the block. Do you think the changes are an improvement? Why?

Buildings are traditionally designed to suit the climate of the area as well as the needs of the people who will live in them. In hot climates, for example, many homes have small windows and thick walls which keep them cool inside. How is the building where you live suited to the climate of your country?

What you can do

Take responsibility for *your* part in the environment. Don't drop litter – use litter bins even if there does seem to be a lot of rubbish around. Encourage your friends to do the same.

Find out what people have done to improve the environment in your area. Join groups who are campaigning for things that interest you. There is a list of addresses on page 32 of this book.

If there is something you feel needs to be done, write a letter to your local paper or to a local government representative to get other people in your area interested.

Buildings

Is there a building site near your home or school? What used to be there? Can you find out what is being built there now?

Some homes are built by employers for their workers. Others are provided by city councils who charge people rent, or built by private developers to sell to people.

Use old maps and photographs from your local library or interview local residents to find out who built the housing in your area and when.

How many different styles of building can you spot around your town or city?

When a lot of homes are built at the same time they all tend to look the same. Carry out a survey of a local street to find out how people have made their homes different from the others. Look out for different-coloured front doors or styles of windows, decorations such as fancy door knockers and different gardens.

During the last one hundred years, new technology and building materials have meant that very tall structures can be built. Today, high-rise buildings made of concrete and metal are common in most cities.

In the 1960s, architects thought that tower blocks would solve the problem of how to create more space in crowded urban areas. But some people think that high-rise living can make people feel isolated and lonely, and encourage vandalism and crime.

▲Architects now realise that it was a mistake to build a network of covered walkways around high-rise tower blocks. The walkways can be frightening and dangerous places to walk alone at night.

Do you live in a block of flats? Who do you think should take responsibility for keeping clean the shared areas such as hallways and stairs?

If someone arrives in a city without a job or can only find work with very low pay, it can be difficult for them to find somewhere to live.

There are homeless people in most cities. Some of these people are forced to sleep outside. Others 'squat' in buildings that are temporarily empty.

Some cities have large shanty towns on their outskirts where people have built their own homes out of whatever materials they can find.

How many public buildings such as libraries or leisure centres do you go into each week? Do they have clear signs outside to tell you what the building is used for? Do they look welcoming? Do they make you want to go inside?

Many older buildings have steep stairs at the entrance or very narrow hallways, making it difficult for people in wheelchairs or people pushing baby buggies to use them.

Buildings and climate

In towns and cities, there are so many buildings close together that it can affect the climate in that area.

Heat escapes from the heating and lighting systems of the buildings and warms up the atmosphere. This escaping heat creates a *microclimate* which is different from the surrounding countryside. The difference is small, but it can still affect the growth and survival of plants and animals.

Insulation

It is expensive to heat and light buildings, so it's important to insulate them to stop heat energy escaping. Which of these brick bonds are used in the walls of the buildings in your neighbourhood?

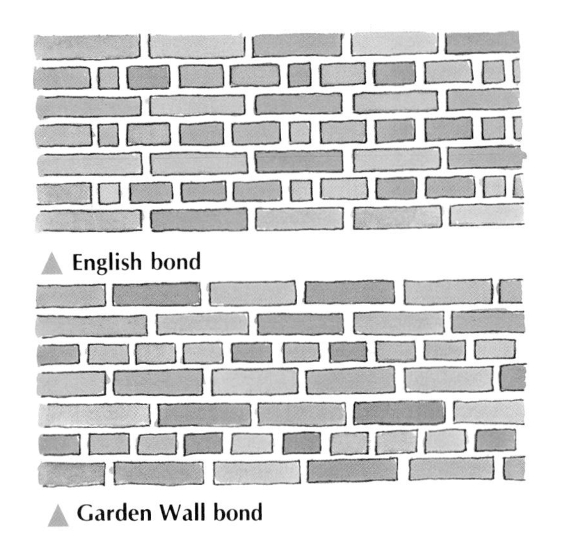

▲ **English bond**

▲ **Garden Wall bond**

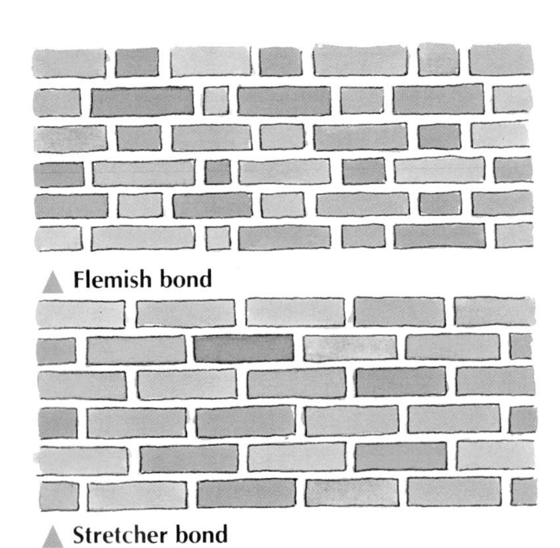

▲ **Flemish bond**

▲ **Stretcher bond**

Stretcher bond is used in the outer layer of a cavity wall. The wall is built in two layers with a space in between which traps the heat.

What other ways are there of insulating buildings?

Transport

Urban areas are full of people moving around, going to school or work, visiting friends or going shopping. A good transport system is important as it helps people to get about easily.

People and transport

Make up a questionnaire to find out the different kinds of transport used by people in your school. Make sure you ask adults *and* children.

Remember to ask questions about:

Where people go and how often they go there.
How far they travel.
What kind of transport they use.
How long it takes them and how much it costs.
Whether the journey is easy or difficult.

Make a graph to show the type of transport which is most often used. Is it the same for children and adults? Does the distance travelled affect the method of transport used? Do you think most people used the best kind of transport for their journey?

When was your street built? Before the end of the 19th century, there were no cars or lorries and people had to walk, or travel in horse-drawn vehicles.

If your area was built before 1900, the roads will probably be quite narrow and the houses will not have garages or driveways. If you live in a new town, the roads will be wider and there will be many places for off-street parking.

► Do you think that the roads which connect these streets of houses would be able to cope with much traffic?

Look in your local library or museum for maps which show your town or city before and after railway lines were built. As the railway system expanded, people could move further away from the city centres and travel in to work by train.

The quieter, cleaner areas on the outskirts of the city centres became known as suburbs. Services such as shops and schools developed to meet the needs of the people living in the suburbs.

Did the arrival of the railways lead to a growth of suburbs in your area?

In developed countries today, people use cars more than any other kind of transport.

However, the narrow streets of old cities were not designed to carry large amounts of traffic. Many places suffer from increasingly long traffic jams, making cars and buses very slow forms of transport. Underground trains can be quicker but often they do not go to all parts of a city.

▶ A car often gives a person with a disability much more freedom. What other reasons are there why people like to use cars?

▼ Traffic jams like this one in Kampala, Uganda are a familiar sight in most of the world's cities.

Plan a journey to the other side of your town. Which is likely to be the quickest route for you to take? Would you have to use more than one method of transport?

The cars that cause traffic jams along the roads of many towns and cities also poison the air with the fumes from their exhaust pipes. Petrol engines produce:

Pollutant	Effect
Carbon monoxide	A gas that prevents enough oxygen being taken into the body. It also causes smogs.
Nitrogen oxides	Gases that cause acid rain and help to create the greenhouse effect which traps the sun's heat, leading to changes in the climate all over the world. These gases also cause breathing problems in humans.
Hydrocarbons	These gases may cause cancer and breathing problems. They help to cause the greenhouse effect.
Carbon dioxide	This gas also helps to cause the greenhouse effect.
Lead	This substance is added to petrol to make cars run more smoothly. It causes health problems, particularly in young children. It is now possible for all new cars to use lead-free petrol and the engines of older cars can be altered to allow them to run on lead-free petrol too.

A device called a catalytic converter or CAT can now be fitted to the exhaust systems of cars which run on unleaded petrol. Chemical reactions inside a CAT change the poisonous gases to much less harmful ones such as carbon dioxide, nitrogen and water vapour. This process reduces the poisonous gases contained in exhaust fumes by up to 90%.

Sixty cars, with one person in each, use about 16 times the amount of energy as a single bus carrying 60 people. Imagine the amount of energy that would be saved if more car drivers travelled by bus instead – as well as the effect this would have on traffic jams!

Each year, many people are killed or injured in road accidents. Find out the road accident figures for your area from your local police station or town hall.

Make your own advertisement

Cut car advertisements out of magazines and watch carefully any that you see on television. What do they tell you about what life would be like if you bought one of the cars being advertised?

Make up a car advertisement of your own showing the other side of the story. Think about traffic jams, pollution and road accidents.

Many cities are trying to find solutions to their traffic problems. In Lagos, Nigeria, only people with certain car registration numbers are allowed to drive into the city on certain days. San Francisco, in the United States, has cut the cost of public transport and provided free car parks on the outskirts of the city.

What do you think of these ideas? Can you think of any other solutions?

In Mexico City, the authorities are trying to reduce air pollution from car exhausts, which is 100 times more than an acceptable level. Each car is given a coloured sticker. On a certain day every week, none of the cars with that colour sticker are allowed to be driven in the city.

Plan the future of transport

This time line from 1850 to the present day shows some of the important events in the history of transport. What would you add to the time line to show the best and worst transport futures you can think of?

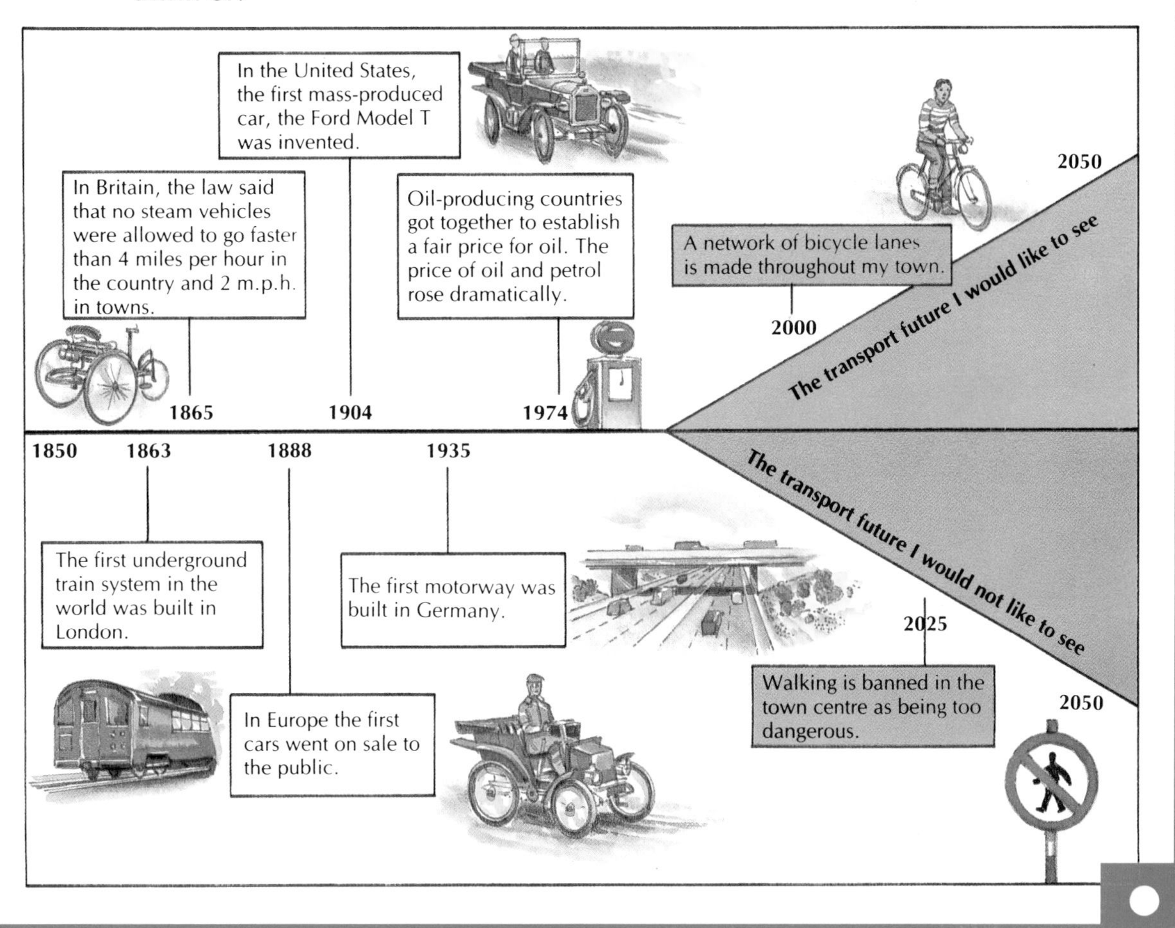

What you can do

Walk or use a bicycle for short journeys rather than travelling by car.

Use public transport when there is a direct, easy route.

Share cars – if you live too far away from school to walk, perhaps your parents and a friend's parents could take it in turns to drive you to school.

Encourage the car drivers you know to use lead-free petrol or have a catalytic converter fitted to their car.

Free time

To stay healthy and happy, everyone needs to relax, to enjoy themselves with friends and to take exercise. In towns and cities where there are large numbers of people living together in one place, spare-time activities have to be specially organised and provided for.

Where do you go in your neighbourhood to relax and have fun? How often do you visit your local library, swimming pool, park or cinema? Do you belong to any clubs?

People and leisure

Make up a questionnaire to find out what leisure facilities other people use in their spare time. Make sure that you ask people of all ages.

Remember to ask questions about:
Where people go for leisure.
How often they go there.
What they do there.
How much it costs.
Whether there is anything else they would like to be able to do.

Make a graph to show which are the most popular activities. Do all groups of people in your area have the leisure facilities they need?

On a map of your local area, mark all the leisure facilities you have found out about. If you could provide for one more kind of free time activity in your area, where would it be needed and who would it be for?

Where do you most enjoy playing? Which of the places where you play are supervised and cleaned? Is there equipment for you to play on? Is it kept in a good state of repair?

Towns and cities often have areas of waste ground where buildings have been knocked down or which have spaces for car parking. Children often use these places as playgrounds. But waste ground, building sites and car parks can be dangerous places and the children who play there risk being involved in serious accidents.

Small towns and villages usually have open spaces round them. Larger towns and cities, need to have parks and public gardens where people can spend their spare time in the open air amongst trees and flowers. Trees also act as 'lungs' for crowded towns and cities because they produce oxygen which we need to breathe.

However, like people, trees find it hard to breathe in areas where the air is dirty and polluted. Dirt from factory smoke and car exhaust fumes blocks up the breathing holes in the leaves of trees.

▶ This aerial photograph shows that some areas of land in Perth, Australia have been left as green spaces and have not been built on.

Research your local park

Sometimes the gardens of houses belonging to rich or powerful people became public parks when the owners died. You can find out the history of your local park by:

Looking for clues around the park such as plaques commemorating events, names or dates on buildings, and so on.

Asking at your local library.

Examining early maps of the local area.

Interviewing the park manager or people who have lived in the area a long time.

Writing a letter to the local paper asking people to send you information about the park.

Waste

Can you remember what you threw away yesterday? How much waste do you think your school produces in one day or your family produces in one week?

▶ This amount of rubbish was produced by a row of market stalls. Fruit and vegetable waste decays naturally without harming the environment, but the materials used to package goods are much more difficult to get rid of.

When a lot of people live in a small area, they produce vast amounts of waste. We throw away more rubbish than our grandparents or great-grandparents. Most of the products we buy are packaged in paper or plastic and when household goods break we tend to throw them away rather than mend them.

Most urban areas have organised systems for waste disposal. Some cities just collect the rubbish and burn it in an incinerator or dump it in pits at landfill sites which are then covered over with earth. In more environmentally-aware cities such as Vienna in Austria and Sheffield in Britain, all household rubbish is taken to a depot where the recyclable materials are sorted into separate containers.

▶ People bring their aluminium cans for recycling to this collection depot in Perth, Australia. Aluminium can be recycled over and over again and each recycled can saves 95% of the energy it would take to make a completely new can.

The journey of rubbish

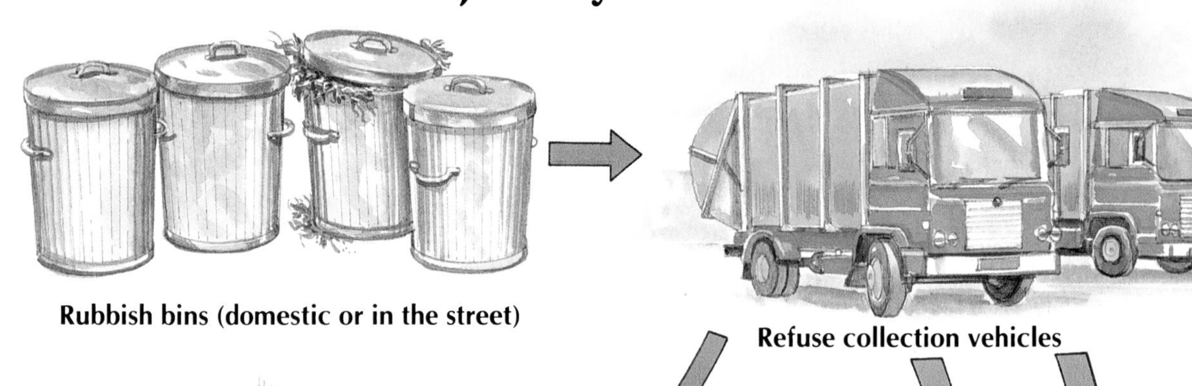

Rubbish bins (domestic or in the street)

Refuse collection vehicles

Incinerator

The rubbish is burnt in large containers at very high temperatures of around 1000 °C. The heat from the burning process can be used to turn water into steam which drives electricity turbines in power stations.

Recycling depot

The rubbish passes along a conveyor belt. Glass, metal, paper, wood and plastic are sorted into different containers to be taken away for recycling.

Landfill site

The rubbish is dumped into large pits in the ground such as disused quarries. Layers of earth are put on top. When the site is full, the land is used for planting or building.

Noise

Crowded cities are often polluted by noise from traffic and machinery.

▶ This Environmental Health officer is testing noise levels in several places in a big city. The inspector investigates complaints from people who think that their lives are being disrupted by noise pollution.

Noise pollution test

Play a tape of music in a quiet side street and then alongside a busy main road. Measure how far away the tape can be heard in each of these places. Record your results for each place and colour code them onto a local map.

Noise insulation test

People working in noisy environments need to wear ear protectors. You could make noise mufflers for your ears using materials such as cotton wool, cloth, newspaper and foam plastic. Test your designs by trying out the mufflers while playing a tape. Measure how far away the sound of the tape can be heard. Record the results on a graph. Which insulating material works best?

Dogs

Although dogs can be good company, they often do not have enough space for exercise in towns and cities. Dog mess is not only unpleasant, it is highly pollutant and carries disease.

Dog owners need to make sure that their animal is walked every day, fed properly and given enough attention for it to be healthy and contented. They should also make sure that they clear up dog mess or train their pet to use dog toilet areas in public parks.

What you can do

Invite an Environmental Health Officer into school to tell you about the ways in which they are responsible for monitoring pollution.

Reuse plastic bags provided by shops when you buy their goods and ask for less packaging when you buy fast food.

Sort out your household waste into materials such as paper, glass bottles and aluminium cans and take them to your local collection site for recycling.

If you have a dog, make sure you clear up the mess it makes when you take it for a walk.

Urban planning

Most towns and cities have developed from groups of small villages over a long time, often following the routes of roads, rivers and railways. Because this kind of 'organic' city grows slowly and gradually, systems of transport and waste disposal are often disorganised and unco-ordinated.

▲ This aerial photograph of Milton Keynes in Britain shows that the city has been planned on a grid system. The land is divided into regular sections which are linked by a network of roads. Each section is used for a different purpose such as housing, leisure or industry.

Some newer cities were carefully planned before being built. Brasilia in Brazil and Milton Keynes in Britain were designed for populations of a certain size and to provide people with things they needed such as car parking space outside homes and public buildings.

Buildings in urban areas need to be connected to a constant supply of water, electricity and gas. A network of underground pipes carries water and gas into people's homes. Electricity travels along cables from the power stations where it is generated to our homes, shops and factories. The cables run underground or hang from huge pylons.

◀ An engineer connects up telephone lines in Abidjan, Ivory Coast. As well as water and power supplies, urban areas need to be linked to a communication network that help people to keep in touch with others, locally, nationally and internationally.

Most towns and cities have planners. Planners carry out surveys and make up questionnaires to find out what people think about new developments in their area. They draw up plans for new projects and decide whether some older buildings or areas should be conserved for people to enjoy.

If there is a need for a new school, hospital or road system, the town planner has to decide where it should be built.

This town planner in El Salvador makes decisions about how new developments will be carried out and about how changes can be made to existing areas.

In many countries today, planners are introducing environmentally-friendly schemes such as recycling centres into urban areas. Energy-efficient houses are being built too, like this one in Sweden. The large windows trap the Sun's energy which is used to heat the house cheaply. The natural insulation provided by the Earth is used to conserve heat in the extra rooms which have been built underground.

Plan a town

Try planning a large town using different-coloured blocks to represent each type of building such as houses, shops and so on. How many people do you think could live in the town?

Make sure that you provide enough housing, facilities for employment, education, leisure and waste disposal. Include a transport system and any other features you think a town should have.

Remember to think about the needs of older and younger people who will be living in your town as well as people with disabilities. Make sure you will be able to explain your plan to other people and justify your planning decisions.

What ideas do you have that might help to improve the lives of people living in towns and cities? Think about what you can do *now* to help to improve the environment where you live.

Useful addresses

If you would like to find out more about the ideas in this book, write to any of these organisations:

Aluminium Can Recycling Association,
1-MEX House, 52 Blucher Street,
Birmingham, B1 1QU.
British Waste Paper Association,
Alexander House Business Centre, Station Road,
Aldershot, Hants. GU11 1BQ.
Council for Environmental Education,
School of Education, University of Reading,
London Road, Reading, RG1 5AG.
Friends of the Earth (UK),
26–28 Underwood Street, London, N1 7JQ.
Friends of the Earth (Australia),
Chain Reaction Co-operative, P.O. Box 530E,
Melbourne, Victoria 3001.
Friends of the Earth (New Zealand),
P.O. Box 39-065, Auckland West.
National Association for Urban Studies,
Canterbury Urban Studies Centre, St Alphege Lane,
Canterbury, Kent, CT1 2EB.
National Society for Clean Air,
136 North Street, Brighton, BN1 1RG.
The Tidy Britain Group,
The Pier, Wigan, WN3 4EX.
UK Reclamation Council,
16 High Street, Brampton, Huntingdon,
Cambridgeshire, PE18 8TU.
Waste Watch,
NCVO, 26 Bedford Square, London, WC1B 3HU.
Women's Environmental Network,
Aberdeen Studios, 22 Highbury Grove, London,
N5 2EA.

Index